Self Hypnosis & For

Inner Peace & Happiness

Robert J Allen

ISBN: 9781521176757

Copyright Egghead Publications 2016
Support@EggheadPublications.co.uk
EggheadPublications.co.uk

Table of Contents

Contents
Title Page

AUTHOR & BOOK BACKGROUND

My Beginning
My Mission
My Result

OBJECTIVE

Objective Summary
Detailed Objective

APPROACH

The Approach Suggested By The Book

SELF HYPNOSIS & VISUALISATION

Self Hypnosis, Relaxation & Visualisation
How And Why Build A Visualisation
Visualisation Attachment
The Role Of Memory
The Role Of Perception, Beliefs & Values
Consider All The Senses
Consider Personality Traits
Example Visualisation With Self Hypnosis
SUBCONSCIOUS
The Subconscious
The Problems With The Subconscious
Resolving The Subconscious Using Visualisation

MINDFULNESS

Example Of Being Mindful
Example Of Not Being Mindful
The Perfect Mindful State
Becoming Naturally Mindful

SELF-IMPROVING VISUALISATIONS CHECKLIST

What Makes Happy People
Right Now I am OK
Being Assertive
Lending & Borrowing & Favours
Self-affirmation & Be Proud of Yourself
Smile
Explore Solutions
Do Your Best & Acceptance
Help Others & Giving
Be Truthful & Honest
Be Humble
Empathy & Walk In Their Shoes
Accept Your Shadow
Addiction & Habits
You Can Only Control So Much
Forgive Yourself
Forgive Others & Let go of Anger & Hate
Letting Go & Drop Burdens
Risk & Pain
Write It Down
Time Heals
Learn From Mistakes
Body Language
Arguments & Less Emotion

VISUALISATIONS TO AVOID CHECKLIST

Texting & Impulse Communication
Over Thinking The Future
Saying Sorry Too Much
Procrastination
Impulse Buying
Judging & Self Reflection
Rushing
Being the Victim
Negative Self-talk
Jealousy
Being Someone Else
Over Caring What People Think

ISSUES & BASIC VISUALISATIONS CHECKLIST

Unhappy, Unwell, Anxious and Depressed
Self-esteem, Self-worth, Self-respect
Lack of Companionship and Good Relations
Bad Friends and Negative People
Shame and Guilt
Jealousy
Nervousness and Shyness
Hate your Job or Life
Always Worrying About What Others Think
No Time and Rushing
Fear
Big Challenges & Breaking Bad Habits
Resentment & Hate
Worry About The Future
Not Liking Yourself
Meeting Targets or Goals
Getting Old
Not Being Attractive

Fear of Taking The First or Next Step
Control and Acceptance

AUTHOR & BOOK BACKGROUND

My Beginning

I could not fully enjoy anything. Even the most gratifying film did not distract me from repeating ill-thoughts. I found it difficult to fall asleep. My disturbed sleep often caused me to wake up, feel terrible and in a cold sweat. Sometimes I woke up and could hardly move because I was so depressed. I could not clean and feed myself. I felt physically ill. I had become fat and I could not walk far without hurting, getting out of breath and sweating. I had unpleasant feelings while tied to a dark ugly gloomy cloud. I spent much time worrying about a hopeless future. With ill feelings, my mind was constantly reflecting and over analysing the past. My behaviour became outrageous, although never unlawful. No matter what I did I was full of regret, shame and guilt. When I was well I found myself rushing and hardly living. Time was rapidly passing in this poor life. There seemed no point in living.

Was the problem serious? My long-term girlfriend dumped me after I attended counselling. The company I worked at made me redundant as I had become an easy non-performing target. I lost the ability to find a new job. I lost all the assets I had built from thirty years in a high paid job. I went bankrupt. I developed a serious drinking problem. I became homeless. I lost all my friends. Only a few of my family supported me. My children did not talk to me because of my negative impact. My behaviour deeply embarrassed me. I wasn't sure whether I had become a 'bad' person. I walked around deeply uncomfortable and depressed. My self-esteem was so low. My ability to cope with life was nearing an end. No one chose to be with me.

I reached 'rock bottom' one Christmas day when I was living in a homeless shelter. It was what most people would consider a beautiful sunny winters day. I sat on a bench, in a public park, facing some badly kept tennis courts with my best friend. We watched happy children playing with their new toys, often with their loving parents. My friend was a serious alcoholic. He was powerless to his addiction and knew it. A huge supply of strong and cheap alcohol lay under the bench. Enough alcohol that would make us happy or at least we thought. Having been a smart suit wearing IT manager and banker, I now looked like a typical person off the streets. I was unclean, dressed in clothes I had gathered from the shelter and felt alien and disconnected. I even feared the police. I was so down.

My mind had become huge building containing many self-made prisons. Subconsciously, all these prisons had entrapped me like an insect trapped in a spider's web.

I suffer from bipolar disorder, I could not continue like this. I was heading for early death. I needed to do something.

<u>If the claw is stuck, the whole bird is lost.
Translated Russian Saying</u>

My Mission

My mission was to free myself, become more peaceful and happy.

I researched, read any book I could find, attended recovery courses and attended Alcoholics Anonymous. I studied ancient and religious texts and own a heap of self-help books and hypnosis media. I even studied scientific papers. I experienced many forms of talking therapies, meditation and hypnosis. My personality had to change. Nothing else would do. Attending injuries with plasters would not heal the deep wounds I had and so 'quick fixes' were not much use.

I have techniques and methods that work for me. I want to share them with you. Are they original? No, but some of the ideas, the whole package, focus and organisation are.

This book is a summary of the techniques and methods I use. The book is about changing personality by addressing and 'correcting' the subconscious. This will slowly cure the rather than just treat the 'symptom'. Ninety percent of your behaviour and beliefs, and thus personality, are subconscious. By definition lack of awareness means that changing the subconscious is a hard undertaking.

In your conscious and subconscious mind you also have a model of the world. This includes a perceived direction that you want to follow, like a map. What if your model and map are wrong? Wouldn't that have serious consequences?

Changing the subconscious will not be easy but every step you take will make you feel better.

<u>True nobility is in being superior to your previous self</u>
Hindustani Proverb

My Result

With my methods and techniques, I continue to improve. I rarely drink and when I do it's social and under control. I am about four stone lighter. My important health signs are excellent. Previously, I needed a 'Continuous Positive Airway Pressure' machine when I slept because of sleep apnoea. I was on much medication, for: mental health, diabetes type 2, cholesterol, sleep, high blood pressure, allergies, muscle and back pain and maybe more. I feel so much better and am a new person that I wish I had always been. I have a good relationship with my children, my friends and family. I am forgiven for my unpleasant past. I am far more confident. My behaviour is improving. I am rebuilding my life. I enjoy my work. The dark gloomy cloud has gone as I have found inner-peace. I am settled and happier than I have ever been.

<u>When there is no enemy within, the enemies outside cannot hurt you</u>
<u>African Proverb</u>

OBJECTIVE

Objective Summary

The purpose of this book and its techniques are to **change your personality** by permanently reprogramming your subconscious.

Over 90% of one's thoughts and behaviours are subconsciously controlled. There are two ways to address the subconscious.

First, to consciously override the subconscious when you recognise it is negatively influencing your life. Nearly all self-help books take this approach. For me, they don't work. I lose interest in consciously overriding my negative thoughts and behaviours. Thus, such techniques do not last long and I return to how I was. Regardless, no deep change occurs to my personality so the experience has to be temporary.

Or, second, to delve into the subconscious and change it. These changes will become natural and so consciously never need to be overridden because there is no negative influence. This has worked for me because my personality has changed for the better.

This book addresses the latter. To change your subconscious so all becomes naturally much healthier without the need of superficial influences on the conscious mind.

The most popular method of changing the subconscious is with the use of audio self-hypnosis material. This is fine and helpful. However, the subjects of this media are broad. The changes made to the subconscious are like a scatter-gun and will only tackle a few of your needs.

This book shows you how to make your own self-hypnosis material that specifically addresses your own needs. It helps and guides you to identify the issues you face. It then explains how to make visualisations to address these issues. Then it leads you into self-hypnosis to make the changes. The methods presented in this book will allow you to create the best self-hypnosis material for you. All will be specifically targeted for your own needs and will cause the greatest beneficial changes.

The personality changes hope to achieve the following:

- Increased Inner Peace
- Increased Happiness & Joy
- Less Anxiety
- Less Depression & Lows
- Increased Purpose & Productivity
- Increased Appreciation of Life

Applying the methods and techniques presented need practise. You cannot run a marathon without training first. You can nearly always improve your performance. The changes will make you more mindful so you make the most out of every moment. You will become much more comfortable with yourself.

Detailed Objective

Quick fixes often need constant conscious thought to apply them. Your subconscious shapes most of your personality. You have limited control on most of the way you present yourself or behave internally. So the subconscious needs to change and for your personality to follow.

Take one common theme. 'Think positive', which on its own, I feel uncomfortable with as I do with shallow 'self-affirmation'. To think positively you have to recognise you are thinking negatively. Then you must change a negative thought to a positive one. It may make a difference for a time but soon you will lose interest in even recognising the negative thoughts let alone replacing them. Have you really become more positive? Have you made a long-term change? Anyway, you are only dealing with a symptom, not the cause which is your personality. It is only by changing some of your personality that anything becomes natural.

The objective of this book is to address root causes by overriding and reprogramming the subconscious. Recognise that your subconscious needs improvement and consciously retrain it by replacing poor personality traits with better ones. The core technique is picturing yourself as you would like to behave and appear. Become a 'new' person that you like and are comfortable with. Both you conscious and subconscious will work in tandem to change your personality for good.

The solution includes:

- Examination of each quality of your personality,
- Identification of all issues and wanted improvements,
- Creation of a detailed picture of how you would like to be,
- Reprogramming the subconscious,
- Doing, and
- Reviewing.

The solution needs many passes and effort. Each time you solve one problem your view and wants will change. Some problems will disappear and need no further work. But previous issues you have addressed may have changed. So with each cycle a review is necessary.

Here is an example of the whole proposed solution cycle as it may be applied. You fear attending meetings. By going through the provided checklists you realise you have a few unwanted personality traits. You picture and foresee yourself as relaxed, not valuing the other attendees as you did before, standing up for yourself and so forth. Then you experience further meetings and all goes much better. Your fear of meetings lessens and your self-esteem grows. Although, you addressed the 'fear of meetings' you have started to address self-esteem. But it is likely that self-esteem is an unwanted trait in other issues you are tackling. So there is a 'snow ball effect' and any prior solutions need review. Some personality traits may have become more important to address than others.

This cycling technique continually changes your personality as your objective to become naturally more mindful, peaceful and happier becomes closer.

APPROACH

The following sections describe the techniques, methods and approach of this book.

The Approach Suggested By The Book

The techniques and methods presented in this book need you to understand the overwhelming power of the subconscious. Challenging the subconscious is key as it is likely to be your enemy. This book contains a dedicated chapter on the subject of the subconscious. Understanding will make it easier to achieve the necessary changes. Read this chapter first.

> Give your enemy a face, If he is human, do not dehumanise him. Know him and know why he is your enemy. If your enemy is within you, understand what it is and why you are afraid. Put a face on your fear. When you understand it, and it is no longer vague and shapeless, you will find that your fear is no longer so formidable."
> Mercedes Lackey

Understanding visualisation and self-hypnosis and how to use them are equally important. It is the key to changing the subconscious. Therefore, this book includes a dedicated chapter on the subject of self-hypnosis and visualisation. Read this chapter second.

> If you can see yourself doing something, you can do it. If you can't see yourself doing something, usually you can't achieve it.
> Seal

There is a dedicated chapter that discusses mindfulness. Mindfulness is recognised as a desirable state for anyone. While this book does not directly teach you to become mindful (there are many books on the subject) you will become naturally more mindful. This is one of the great benefits of following the approach and methods in this book.

The remaining chapters discuss the approach.

Using the designed checklists will help identify the changes you want. There is no need to print or complete these checklists but some people may prefer this. The checklists cover many subjects a trained consultant or counsellor would cover. Everyone faces similar issues and want similar improvements. The checklists provoke you to come up with ideas about the issues you uniquely face. The lists are not complete because everyone is different. The checklists will spark ideas of your own to address your specific issues and create your own visualisations.

The basic technique addresses issues of the subconscious to create favourable change in yourself using visualisation. Bold capitalised words in the checklists have detailed sections dedicated to them. These subjects cover shared topics throughout the book.

There are three checklists. One is about identifying the specific issues you face and basic visualisations to overcome them. The second checklist covers visualisations you should avoid. The third checklist covers general improvements that you should try to achieve.

The picture below illustrates the basic approach. The picture represents one big process with several smaller processes. The whole 'big' process repeats until the desired changes have occurred. The coloured boxes represent smaller steps. These steps follow the order from the top to bottom. There is one wrapping and cycling process called 'Review'. At the end of the 'big' process, some changes will have occurred so the next cycle will need changing too.

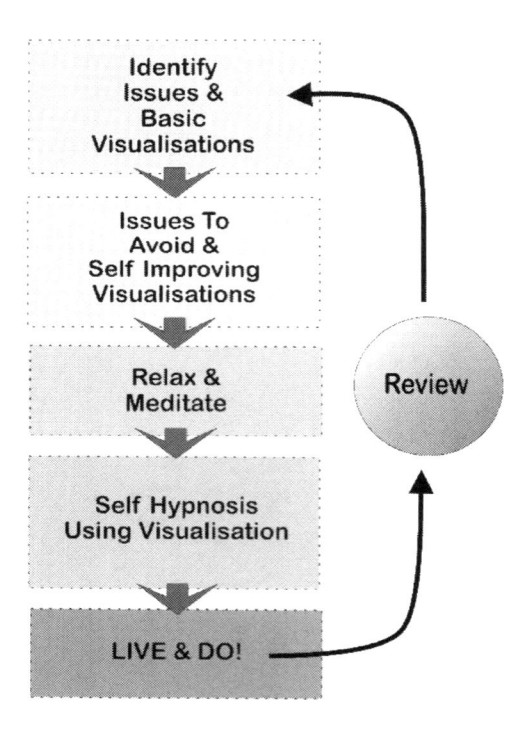

```
Identify Issues & Basic Visualisations
        ↓
Issues To Avoid & Self Improving Visualisations
        ↓
Relax & Meditate  →  Review
        ↓
Self Hypnosis Using Visualisation
        ↓
LIVE & DO!  ────┘
```

1. Identify the issues you have, the ones that bother you or you know need improving and picture how they could improve. The **ISSUES & BASIC VISUALISATIONS CHECKLIST** found later aims to provoke identification of the issues you face and how to picture improvements.

Please remember, you must also elaborate to find issues not mentioned in the text for a greater change.

2. Identify more improvements you would like to make to address the topics in step 1. There are issues and visualisations you should avoid. The **VISUALISATIONS TO AVOID CHECKLIST** provides a guide.

3. Build a detailed picture of the 'improved you' using both the issues and the improvements you would like to make. This visualisation is an imaginary picture of how you would like to be. The **SELF-IMPROVING VISUALISATIONS CHECKLIST** will help you discover the improvements you would like to make. Again, although the book suggests many areas of improvement you could include your own. Create a picture of your: behaviour, thoughts, feelings and so forth. With this full imaginary picture, you are ready to move on.

4. It is time to prepare yourself to use your visualisation to start changing your subconscious. It is important to relax your mind as much as possible. To relax take a warm bath, sit comfortably and quietly or use a method of your own choosing. The best results use meditation. When you have reached a relaxed state it is time to experience your visualisation. See yourself feeling, thinking, experiencing and changing using the picture you created in step 4.

5. An important step is then to experience real-life where the earlier issues arise. This is the "DO" phase. Not only is this important to deeply embed changes but by experiencing the benefits you will gain confidence in the whole approach.

6. You will have gained full or partial success. If it is a partial success you need to review the 'new you'. Perhaps, you now need to change the process because you missed further benefits. Resolving some of the issues will allow you to focus on the more stubborn matters. Also, if you have a collection of checklists any change may have a domino effect and they need review too.

The whole process will become easier, the issues will become less and the techniques and methods will become increasingly powerful. Changes will become deeply rooted in your subconscious.

SELF HYPNOSIS & VISUALISATION

Visualisation is the main technique proposed in this book to change the subconscious. Therefore, it is necessary to say much more about it.

Most top sportsmen and women use visualisation to advance their performance. Take a golfer, for instance, who has missed a few vital putts in major competitions. Picturing being relaxed, taking the putt as if no one was looking and so forth has made a great difference to some golfers. However, one warning about visualisation, scientific research suggests there is little value in seeing yourself achieving your ultimate goal or dream without considering how you get there. In other words, there is no point visualising your ideal partner, the way they look, the money they have or how you get on. There is no point in seeing yourself in a great house by the countryside with fancy cars. There is no point in visualising the day you get that much wanted promotion you wanted. In fact, it can be harmful visualising a goal and failing.

Visualisation can help the **process** of getting to your goal and retrain your subconscious. With the golfer there was little point in picturing holding a trophy in the air, being champion and rocketing up the world-ranking. However, visualisation could help with the **process** of putting. Like the golfer, improving little processes will increase the chance of achieving the overall goal.

Another example, you need great qualifications for your choice university. You have upcoming exams. There is no point seeing yourself four weeks after the exams getting the grades you need. However, visualising yourself working hard, employing good study habits and being great at preparing yourself for the exams will help. It is the process that you can improve by visualisation to make yourself more likely to achieve your goal.

Self Hypnosis, Relaxation & Visualisation

Remove the idea that self-hypnosis is about taking a gold watch out of your pocket and staring at it as it swings in the air. Self-hypnosis is the act of becoming deeply relaxed, concentrating on a visual and imaginary picture (visualisation) and letting the mind become more receptive to suggestions. This is how you can touch the subconscious and permanently change it.

Most of this book focuses on the suggestions that are to be introduced to your mind using visualisation while being in a hypnotic state. The state of mind you want to achieve is a pre-sleep mind wondering state. For instance, the state: just before sleep, on a long journey in a car as it rocks and makes you sleepy or when you go for a long walk. Meditation is perfect and there are many books on this subject.

I will briefly cover one of my favourite and common relaxation techniques. Some people call it the 'body scan'. Sit or lie in a comfortable position. Close your eyes. Start with your right foot. Notice, as much as is possible, how your foot feels. Notice the feelings of your toes touching each other. Notice any aches or tension. Notice the temperature and the feelings of your sock against the skin. Notice, are there are any colours associated with the foot. Notice how your foot feels now. For two seconds tighten and scrunch up the foot. Notice the tension, the effort and possible discomfort. Relax. NOTICE THE DIFFERENCE BETWEEN relaxed and tense. Repeat the tension and relax process two further times.

The objective is to now move around the body. So you do the same with the: left foot, right ankle, left ankle, calves, knees, thighs, bottom, waist, chest, lower back, upper back, fingers, wrist, lower arms, upper arms, shoulders, neck, mouth, cheeks, area around the eyes, brow and so forth.

Once you have gone around the body just lie or sit there. Imagine that you have slipped into a warm bath and let the new feeling of the body relaxation spread across your body. Listen to the sounds around you and focus on each of them. You are now ready to visualise and are in a hypnotic state. REMEMBER, when you notice your mind has wondered as it will do, gently bring it back and focus on your breathing. Some people also like to imagine there is a trapdoor on the top of the head and imagine any unwanted thoughts floating out of the head.

You can do the body scan any time. After practise you can do it all in your head. I have reached the stage where I can easily remember the relaxed state and introduce it without effort.

Visualisation is a mental process. You create an imaginary picture of a future event or situation. How will you behave? What will you see? What will you feel? What will you think? The more detailed the vision the better. Then you rehearse the event as you imagined it in your mind in a relaxed state. You achieve this by sitting quietly, lying down, meditating, just before sleep or as previously described. You then imagine you are living the visualisation.

Visualisation changes your subconscious making natural and permanent to your personality.

It is important to associate the imaginary picture to something that will trigger the vision's thoughts and feelings. This could just be the event. However, it is often better to attach a single mental image you can recall easily. It can even be a sound or smell. For instance, if the event is a meeting have a colourful photograph in your mind where you are smart, comfortable, relaxed, with a notebook and smiling.

The following is an example of a visualisation. See how you can influence your subconscious with this experiment. If it does not immediately work for you do not worry and keep trying. If it does work you will see that change is possible. Each rehearsal will achieve better results.

Think and picture a "green horse". A horse standing still, painted in a single dark shade of green. There are no emotions and no thoughts associated with this imaginary picture although you might think it is a little odd.

Now imagine this or something similar. The green horse is galloping gracefully around a pen of short green flowing grass. You are in the countryside and feeling relaxed. Although the horse is green you can see its magnificent muscles stretch and strain under the slight sheen of sweat. You can smell pollen. You can gently feel the autumn sun on your arms and face. You have had a good day. You have completed all your chores and you are free to relax. You are going to watch your favourite TV programme tonight and eat your favourite meal. What is more, you have a day off work tomorrow and your children are away with your parents. Your comfortable warm soft bed is ready to welcome you when you sleep.

It is time to relax and use your visualisation. Quietly, close your eyes and concentrate and picture this scene for several minutes before you read further. Try to remove any other thoughts by letting them drift away. Give yourself time and immerse into your visualisation, like slipping into a warm bath. See yourself smiling and enjoying the experience. Feel the relaxing warm sensation. Let the great feelings spread throughout your body.

Let some time pass, maybe do something. Now think and picture a green horse. You will find the green horse image now comes with some emotions and thoughts. You have influenced your subconscious. You will instantly recall these without effort. I bet you cannot think of a green horse without attaching new thoughts and feelings to it. This is a way to re-program your subconscious mind.

> The way to get rid of darkness is with light; the way to overcome cold is with heat; the way to overcome the negative thought is to substitute the good thought. Affirm the good, and the bad will vanish.
> Joseph Murphy

How And Why Build A Visualisation

The main checklists in this book will allow you to build the skeleton of your visualisation. Flesh needs adding to make it complete and compelling. A full and realistic visualisation makes the most powerful imprint on your subconscious.

You need to build a picture beforehand so it is easy to put it into practise. Building visualisations first also ensures that you have thought about everything. Just the act of building will introduce improvements too.

So how do you add flesh to the skeleton visualisation that you have already built? You need to bear in mind many further factors to include in your build. Discussions on these items follow in the remaining sections of this chapter.

But in summary, it is important to:
- Make sure the visualisation can be easily triggered and remembered
- Understand why memory is an important addition to your picture
- Understand why perception needs consideration
- How to build your senses into your picture to make it realistic
- What facets of your personality you should look at.

With the full picture, you have now built you have the greatest chance of a successful visualisation to get the best results.

Visualisation Attachment

Wouldn't it be nice when you are walking down the road and something triggers your visualisation and brings about all the good thoughts and feelings you previously worked on? Also, would it not be equally good that with one memory you can trigger better thoughts and feelings? This is why having good triggers for your visualisations are important. If you work hard at the techniques and methods in this book triggers will naturally occur. Nevertheless, it is important to have the best triggers to set off visualisations so like a fire they continually spread and become more of your life.

Most of us know that we can catch a whiff of a smell that brings back lucid memories. The brain processes odours and memories and triggers the subconscious. Smells go to your olfactory bulb, a region in your brain that analyses odours. This area of the brain connects to your amygdala and hippocampus. These are regions of the brain that handle memory and emotion. Over time you have subconsciously associated the smell with events, scenes and feelings. This is similar to the results you will get from building and practising your own visualisations. The only difference is that you will make your own triggers.

How do you make and attach something to a visualisation? The sections that follow 'memory' and 'senses' will explain fully. But you need to build an icon like you might have on a computer. Although this icon is a picture it will have words, smells, feelings and so forth. This is all simply a bite-sized visualisation that encapsulates a greater picture. Again the more this boxes a visualisation in a simple form the better. Soon you will find a smell, an image, a feeling, a thought, a picture and so forth will automatically bring about the benefits of your visualisation. This is the power of the subconscious now working in your favour.

The Role Of Memory

The mind likes outrageous images, strange stories, odd movement and so forth and ignores the ordinary and the mundane. Nothing to the mind is duller than words, a phrase or sentence. We remember images, routes, places and pictures far better than we do words. This is why some people can quickly scan a deck of playing cards and remember them and their order. No one who successfully memorises decks in this way uses words. They often associate a picture of something with each card. One of the Grand Masters of Memory uses famous people to represent each card. Each number and suit have meaning too. For instance, a diamond-suited card is a rich celebrity, a heart-suited card is one that he loves and so forth. The numbers have meaning too, for instance, a Ten can mean a 'top celebrity' whereas a Jack may mean a 'religious figure'. The order is often remembered by taking a journey or using a place. Using a mansion as your place, you may go through the rooms as you follow a route through the house.

An example of this technique might be as follows. The third card you see is the Ten of Hearts, your favourite celebrity is Eddie Murphy. The third room you enter is the kitchen. So you see Eddie Murphy in the Kitchen. Perhaps, to make it more memorable you see him chopping the biggest carrot you have ever seen.

I hope you get the idea. You can see this will be more effective than trying to remember the card and its order without images, routes, places and so forth. It is worth researching memory methods and finding one that suits you. I rarely write lists these days as I can create a visual memory just as successfully. So using memory techniques can help you in daily life. If you have children it is an excellent method for revising for exams and tests.

Why is memory so important for visualisation? First, a better memory of the visualisation you build the more easily you will be able to make sure you use it to the full. Second, when you build the visualisation more information will firmly enter your subconscious. Finally and most importantly, the replay of all thoughts and feelings will be easily triggered and recalled. It replaces a bad record with a powerful new one. This is just what you want.

The Role Of Perception, Beliefs & Values

We mentally model the world around us. We model the world and judge events and situations based on our previous experiences. This is why two people may see an event, person or situation completely differently. We even have mental maps of where we are and where we want to go. Have you ever considered that your map, route or destination may be wrong? Our perspectives are often subconscious.

It is important to question your perspective all the time while building any visualisation. As you build a visualisation question your perspective. Often when building you will realise that your perspective could be shaky. If you discover your perspective is not right it is important to correct it. Correcting and changing ones perspective is key to addressing the subconscious.

Imagine you are walking down the street and you see a man that is so drunk he can hardly walk. His clothes look shabby and unclean, he is unshaven and his hair is unkempt. You might think to yourself he is a disgrace, his whole life has long been a mess, he is an alcoholic and so forth. This view came from your preconceived perspective.

But see how your perspective will change when I tell you that his two-year-old drowned in a bath two weeks ago. He thought it was his fault because he thought he had shut the bathroom door and was only on the phone for a few minutes. His wife is now in hospital having tried to commit suicide. Your opinion, attitude and judgement were clearly wrong. What is more, there was no real evidence that suggested that you should have had your first opinion.

Be careful with perception because it is often wrong. Be aware of this when you build a visualisation.

Consider All The Senses

Senses are important to become mindful but equally influential in visualisation. If you consider all your senses you will make your visualisations more complete.

For example, you might want to picture yourself as relaxed. It may help to feel cool, feel the comfortable seat below you and smell fresh air in a silent atmosphere. These feelings add to the visualisation.

We are all aware we have five senses. However, recent research suggests that we may have up to twenty.

Consider incorporating the listed senses, below, into all of your visualisations.

- Colour
- Bright or darkness
- Taste
- Smell
- Sweetness taste and smell
- Saltiness taste and smell
- Sourness taste and smell
- Bitterness taste and smell
- Savoury taste and smell
- Touch rough, smooth, cool and so forth
- Pressure of touch
- Itch
- Temperature
- Sound
- Body awareness

- Tension high or low
- Pain or lack of pain
- Skin
- Bones & Joints
- Body Organs
- Balance
- Internal Well-Being
- Thirst or lack of thirst
- Hunger or fullness
- Time

As you visualise it is best to imagine how any relevant senses feel to convince your mind of the new picture.

Consider Personality Traits

We relate to the world around us and reveal ourselves to other people as our personality. Our personality remains mainly in the subconscious and what people see are our actions and nature. In our mind personality drives our thoughts, beliefs and values that cause this behaviour. There are facets of our personality that we would like to change. Indeed, we may start to create a visualisation to address them. We should be proud of our good personality traits. Use self-affirmation to reinforce these great traits to focus on the positives.

To build a full visualisation the more you detail the personality facets you want to change the better. The list below will help jolt your mind so you can consider and select traits to complete your visualisation.

Abrasive
Abrupt
Active
Adaptable
Admirable
Adventurous
Aggressive
Agreeable Disagreeable
Alert
Aloof
Amiable
Ambitious Unambitious

Amoral
Amusing
Angry
Anxious
Apathetic
Appreciative Unappreciative
Argumentative
Arrogant
Articulate
Artificial
Aspiring
Assertive Unassertive
Athletic
Attractive
Authoritarian
Balanced
Bizarre
Bland
Blunt
Brave Cowardly
Brilliant
Brutal
Calculating
Callous
Calm
Cantankerous
Capable
Capitalistic
Captivating
Careless
Caring
Casual
Cautious
Challenging
Charitable Uncharitable

Charismatic
Charming Charmless
Cheerful
Childish
Circumspect
Clumsy
Cold
Colourful
Compassionate
Competitive
Complacent
Complex
Conceited
Confident
Confidential
Conscientious
Conservative
Considerate Inconsiderate
Constant
Contemplative
Contented Discontented
Contemptible
Conventional
Convincing Unconvincing
Cooperative Uncooperative
Courageous
Course
Courteous
Crafty
Crass
Crazy
Creative Uncreative
Critical Uncritical
Crude
Cruel

Cultured
Curious
Cynical
Daring
Debonair
Decent
Deceptive
Decisive Indecisive
Dedicated
Delicate
Demanding
Desperate
Destructive
Determined
Devious
Difficult
Dignified
Directed
Disciplined Undisciplined
Disciplined
Disconcerting
Discouraged
Discreet
Disruptive
Dogmatic
Domineering
Dramatic
Dreamy
Driving
Droll
Dry
Dull
Dutiful
Dynamic
Earnest

Educated
Efficient
Egocentric
Elegant
Eloquent
Emotional
Empathetic
Energetic
Enquiring
Enthusiastic
Envious
Erratic
Excitable
Expedient
Extraordinary
Extravagant
Fair
Faithful
False
Familiar
Fanatical
Fanciful
Fearful
Feminine
Fickle
Fiery
Firm
Flamboyant
Flexible
Focused
Focused Aimless
Foolish
Forceful
Forgetful
Forgiving

Formal
Forthright
Freethinking
Friendly Unfriendly
Frightening
Frivolous
Frugal
Fun-loving
Gallant
Generous
Gentle
Genuine
Glamourous
Gloomy
Good-natured
Graceful Graceless
Grateful Ungrateful
Greedy
Gullible
Hardworking
Hateful
Healthy
Hearty
Helpful
Heroic
Hesitant
Honest Dishonest
Honourable
Hostile
Humble
Humorous
Idealistic
Ignorant
Ill-mannered
Imaginative Unimaginative

Impatient
Impersonal
Impressionable
Impressive Unimpressive
Impulsive
Incisive
Independent
Individual
Indulgent
Inhibited
Innovative
Inoffensive
Insightful
Intelligent
Intense
Intuitive
Irritable
Kind
Knowledgeable
Lazy
Liberal
Logical
Loud
Lovable
Loyal Disloyal
Malicious
Masochistic
Masculine
Maternal
Mature
Mechanical
Mellow
Messy
Methodical
Meticulous

Miserable
Misguided
Moderate
Modest
Money-Minded
Moody
Morbid
Mystical
Narcissist
Narrow-minded
Neat
Neglectful
Neurotic
Naive
Neutral
Obedient Disobedient
Objective
Obnoxious
Observant
Obsessive
Odd
Offhand
Old Fashioned
One-Dimensional
Open
Opinionated
Opportunistic
Optimistic
Orderly
Organised
Original
Outrageous
Outspoken
Painstaking
Paranoid

Passionate
Passive
Patient Impatient
Patriotic
Peaceful
Perceptive
Perfectionist
Personable
Persuasive
Presumptuous
Perverse
Petty
Placid
Playful
Plodding
Pompous
Popular
Possessive
Practical
Practical Impractical
Precise
Prejudiced
Prim
Principled
Private
Profound Shallow
Progressive
Protective
Proud
Providential
Prudent Imprudent
Punctual
Purposeful
Quiet
Quirky

Rational
Reactive
Realistic Unrealistic
Reflective
Relaxed
Reliable Unreliable
Religious
Repressed
Resentful
Reserved
Resourceful
Respectful Disrespectful
Responsible Irresponsible
Responsive
Retiring
Ridiculous
Rigid
Ritualistic
Romantic
Rustic
Sanctimonious
Sadistic
Sarcastic
Scheming
Scholarly
Scornful
Scrupulous
Secretive
Secure Insecure
Sedentary
Self Conscious
Self Indulgent
Self-critical
Self-defacing
Self-denying

Selfless Selfish
Self-reliant
Self-sufficient
Sensitive
Sensual
Sentimental
Serious
Sharing
Short-sighted
Shrewd
Shy
Silly
Simple
Sincere Insincere
Single Minded
Skillful
Sloppy
Slow
Sly
Sociable
Soft
Solid
Solitary
Sophisticated
Spontaneous
Sporting
Stable Unstable
Steady
Stern
Strict
Strong Willed
Stubborn
Studious
Stylistic
Suave

Subjective
Subtle Blunt
Submissive
Superficial
Superstitious
Sweet Nasty
Sympathetic
Systematic
Tasteful
Thorough Messy
Thoughtless
Tidy
Timid
Tolerant
Tough
Transparent
Troublesome
Trusting Untrusting
Caring Uncaring
Uncomplaining
Understanding
Upright
Venturesome
Vivacious
Vulnerable
Warm
Weak
Weak Willed
Well-bred
Well-meaning
Well-read
Well-rounded
Winner
Wise Stupid
Wishful

Witty
Youthful

Example Visualisation With Self Hypnosis

Take a moment and picture you are going out for a date. You are nervous and predicting you will be apprehensive and boring. Go through all the senses and imagine yourself as more positive, interesting and suitably adjust your body language.

You might picture the night before negatively. You are sweating mildly. The date is a person that won't like you. You are holding your body awkwardly and your walk appears unnatural. The table will be found in a busy area with loud people. The lights will be bright and show every facial blemish and cause your eyes to go red. You won't feel well and you won't be in the mood. Your body will be clammy. You won't know what to say and your humour will dry up. Even though the meal might be one of your favourites you won't be hungry. This is negative self-talk and is an unfavourable visualisation. This will make it more likely that all will go wrong. If the date does not work out it will further convince you that you are a failure.

This negative view can be addressed through an improved visualisation by changing the way you see the date going. You can persuade your subconscious that all will go well. With practise you either won't worry about the date at all or at least you will see it more positively before it happens. You could see yourself relaxed. There is a quiet table at the back of the restaurant where you know you will be comfortable. The light will be dim and possibly lit by candlelight. The seat will be comfortable. The temperature will be perfect. When your date arrives you will enjoy getting to know them. You feel well and this is just the way you would like to spend tonight. You are hungry and are about to eat one of your favourite meals which you will appreciate regardless. What ever happens it will be a good experience and may have a great outcome. Anyway, if the person doesn't like you does it really matter what they think. With this visualisation, it is less likely that anything will go wrong. If something does go wrong you will have a healthier perspective. If most of the event goes right your subconscious and conscious thoughts will become more positive.

This is the power of visualisation. When you start you may have difficulty seeing and feeling your new visions. With practise all becomes easier. Your ability to visualise and positively persuade your subconscious will become increasingly effective. Also, your confidence in the techniques will grow. Your subconscious will slowly become more positive without you realising it. With enough positive experiences, all apprehension will slowly evaporate. You will simply react to events when they occur and not earlier. In fact, you will become more mindful. This is natural mindfulness.

SUBCONSCIOUS

The following sections discuss the subconscious, what it is, why it is important, why change is needed and how to make these changes.

The Subconscious

It is important to appreciate the power of the subconscious to change and re-program it. Knowing it affects most of our nature and behaviour will benefit change.

The subconscious comprises of several layers, according to experts. This book will simplify the mind into two layers, the conscious and the subconscious. The conscious mind consists of thoughts we are aware of. The subconscious is simply brain activity that occurs without our knowledge.

Our basic DNA is present at birth and seemingly can change. From our basic biological nature, our subconscious grows.

All living organisms have pre-programmed needs. We need to survive. We need a way to obtain energy. We need to reproduce and so forth. As each basic requirement is met we develop higher needs. Eventually, we may want friends, clothes, gadgets, money and so forth.

We develop beliefs and values. No one knows what is caused by biology or environment. It would be fair to assume both are major factors as there is evidence for both.

We experience events. Our experience is flavoured by our pre-programming, beliefs, values and our past. Most of this flavouring originates from our subconscious.

Again the experienced events alter the subconscious. It is a never-ending cycle that grows ever deeper.

> Everyone is kneaded out of the same dough but not baked in the same oven.
> Yiddish proverb

According to experts about 90 percent of our brain activity occurs in our subconscious. After a time we build a subconscious model of the world we perceive. We build many internal prisons that we find difficult to free ourselves from. We develop a map of where we are and where we think we should go. We develop values, beliefs, attitudes and behaviour to live our best. We develop negative views of ourselves and keep repeating the same mistakes without understanding. This is our core personality. Of course, all of our individual models, perceptions and subconscious thoughts are faulty. They are only wrong when they limit your happiness and cause unnecessary suffering. Even after much work, our world model will never be perfect. However, our world model and map can be greatly improved. Each model correction will deeply change your personality, become a habit and greatly improve your life.

Many of us have learnt to drive and to understand the Highway Code. The learning process needed effort and practise. It took time to control the car. It took time to understand the road rules. It took time to understand all the signs and road markings. It took time to gain confidence.

But once you had learnt all these skills they moved into the subconscious. If you are an experienced driver then you know most of the time you are rarely aware of your driving. In fact, when you drive you can happily talk to someone, think, worry and so forth.

But, like many of us, soon a few bad habits come into play. Maybe you have started to cross your hands when you use the steering wheel. Maybe you have stopped using the rear-view mirror as much as you should. You did not want to introduce these bad habits but they too have become subconscious. You are not aware of them unless you consciously check how you are driving.

If someone asks for your telephone number where do you get it from? You consciously have to delve somewhere to recover it. You have a vast internal database. The subconscious does not merely contain knowledge but also behaviours, feelings, actions, thoughts and so forth.

Emotions and feelings shape the subconscious mind as much as physical feelings and thoughts. Emotional pain is like physical pain. Holding your hand over a flame hurts so you don't do it again. You get emotionally upset when a friend will not talk to you anymore. You will avoid acting like you did again. Our emotions are a defence to avoid emotional pain. All thoughts, feelings, behaviour arising from the subconscious are to ensure the best action is taken when faced with a similar set of circumstances. This stimulus-action process moves into the subconscious. Learnt actions and thoughts become subconscious and with the slightest stimulation replay, like a record, without question.

We have evolved to remove as much conscious effort so we can focus on new challenges. A new challenge might be to make a fish net for the first time needed to satisfy your hunger.

The subconscious is important because it creates feelings and thoughts we don't want. Feelings come from the subconscious without you being aware. Uncomfortable feelings are unwelcome as they often don't come with their underlying thoughts and reasoning. The subconscious explains the origin of dark and gloomy feelings that come from nowhere.

This book does not recommend avoidance it promotes change. Simply becoming more aware of yourself, your feelings and your mind will start the healing process. But then visualisation will dramatically change the subconscious.

The Problems With The Subconscious

What is the problem with the subconscious? All of our actions, feelings, behaviours and so forth impact any new experiences and enjoyment of this moment. We are unaware of stimulating events and our resulting reactions. Even if we are aware, like picking a cup of the table you cannot consciously recall all the steps and moves needed. Some of our internal thoughts and reactions will be faulty and unreasonable. What is worse is the faults build layer on layer. An early fault starts to make the whole mind unstable.

What are faults? A subconscious fault is one that later causes you to suffer or not enjoy the moment in some way. Why are there faults? We cannot help it. We are all biologically different. We lose brain cells and neural connections. Our memories develop inaccuracies. We interpret events differently. Our choice of a suitable action might not be the best, yet we will continue to repeat it until we learn otherwise.

The difficulty with matters of the subconscious mind is identifying what is wrong and even what is there. The checklists contained in this book address this in detail. Your mind, your knowledge and behaviours are boundless and complex. For instance, just how big is that internal database you managed to get your telephone number from? There are skills and knowledge that are attained without any work. Most of us need effort to remember a telephone number. When first presented with the telephone number it consciously has to be saved to the subconscious to remember it. Similarly, bad habits caused by the subconscious need conscious effort for change.

Resolving The Subconscious Using Visualisation

Influencing our subconscious needs some action from our conscious mind. If you can identify a specific issue you can go straight to it. However, the checklists contained in this book will help you identify your own issues. Still, we may not understand the origin of our thoughts and behaviours. Any fixes have to act like a broad-spectrum antibiotic where some of the cause is unknown. Some issues will reveal themselves as you work and others will remain hidden. Unfortunately, that is the nature of the subconscious.

We have all had bad experiences. Our evolution dictates that survival is of the utmost importance. We have a deep need to protect ourselves so we probably learn from bad experience more than any other. However, we often lose perspective of what actually happened and what we should have learnt. Instead, we learn the wrong lessons.

For example, I once stepped off the pavement and a car hit me. I have never felt such an awesome and powerful impact. My life changed for some time. I developed a fear of going out because I could not get anywhere without crossing the road. It started to become a phobia. This was the wrong lesson to learn, it was illogical.

What should I have learnt? I should have learnt that stepping off the pavement without looking is dangerous. My behaviour needed to change to look before stepping onto the road. What did I learn? It is dangerous to go out because I will have to cross roads. My behaviour changed and for a time I did not go out. It is clear the experience lead to false thinking. The bad experience affected my daily life. This is not a suitable reaction.

> <u>Experience is a hard teacher because she gives the test first, the lesson afterwards.</u>
> <u>Vernon Law</u>

To introduce better thinking repetitive visualisation will make changes natural so they need no further effort. The subconscious can be stubborn and hold firmly to old thoughts and feelings. Past events need to have a healthy perspective. Our overall attitude needs to change and be positive. All this will transform us to become free to enjoy the moment, find inner peace and greater happiness.

MINDFULNESS

Example Of Being Mindful

You wake up peaceful on your day off. Rested, you are free of unpleasant feelings and fully at ease. You have done a hard week's work and you feel good. You are free of care. You feel the cool bedsheet under you with the warm duvet above you. You feel the soft texture of the bedcover. You feel the fresh morning air as a gentle breeze flows across your face. You can smell the gentle fragrance of the blooming flowers outside. In the distance, you hear the soft chirping of lively birds. You notice the sunshine beaming through the clear and clean window. You are looking forward to the day. You are enjoying the moment.

Wouldn't you want to feel like this most of the time? You are naturally mindful as you did not try to feel like this.

Example Of Not Being Mindful

In the morning you woke up and were naturally mindful. You were comfortable, happy and enjoying the moment. There were no thoughts about the past and little about the future. Later in the afternoon, you are with your family beside a lake. Nothing has changed but you are not aware of the cool air sweeping your face, the gentle rippling blue water or the small darting fish in the shallows. You don't even notice the beautiful white swan gracefully swim by. You are tense and not aware of your thoughts. Your mind is muggy. Where have the morning's peaceful feelings gone? You are no longer naturally mindful.

In the afternoon, you could consciously try becoming more mindful to improve your state of mind as you learnt how. Being naturally mindful would have avoided this need.

The Perfect Mindful State

So what would the perfect mindful state look like? I saw a picture of a tiger facing imminent death. There were aggressive men holding spears rapidly approaching the tiger entrapped in a pit. The tiger clutched the side of the pit with its claws deeply buried in the muddy wall. At the bottom of the pit protruded many sharp sticks. The tiger would die if it fell, he would die if he managed to clamber out. The tiger was smiling. Strange? He was living in the present. This moment, right now the tiger was happy. His thoughts were not in the future or the past. I imagine he was admiring the flowers that grew near the pit, the stretching feeling in his muscles and the soil and grass between his claws.

Becoming Naturally Mindful

Can a leopard change its spots? In other words, can you permanently change your **whole** personality? I suggest not because when born some of your personality already exists. Almost immediately after birth identical twins differ. For instance, by nature one twin might be quiet and the other verbose. I am shy, so shy I could not even look into adult's eyes until I was eighteen. I am now outgoing because of the methods I used throughout my life. Friends, acquaintances and family would say that I am close to an extrovert. I have treated my shyness because deep down I am still shy. I have merely blurred one of my leopard spots.

Another question is, can one uphold a permanent mindful state? I have spoken to a couple of Buddhist monks. Interested, I asked if they spent their whole time in a mindful state. Not only do these monks specifically tackle mindfulness and meditate but they train their thoughts to be healthy and positive. Both of them said no. If Buddhist monks cannot stay mindful all the time then I would suggest nor can the average person. One can increase the depth and frequency of your mindful experience but no more.

Finally, can the change to your personality be permanent? To this, I say a resounding yes. Let me give you a simple example. Let us say meetings terrify you. The cause of the terror is a lack of confidence, self-esteem and high self-consciousness. You read this book and apply the methods and techniques. With all the issues adequately addressed soon you attend meetings without much thought. What happens? First, meetings do not pose a problem anymore and that is a permanent change. What is more, because you have successfully conquered a fear you self-confidence and self-esteem will rise. These were the original issues that caused difficulty to start with, so in turn will reduce any further apprehension. You see the change perpetuates. As reversing the change is no longer possible the change becomes permanent. So permanent that one day meetings will not trouble you. In fact, you may learn to enjoy them.

SELF-IMPROVING VISUALISATIONS CHECKLIST

The following sections include general themes that you should try to include in your visualisations. You should use this as a checklist to make sure your whole visualisation has a positive effect.

What Makes Happy People

Research suggests the happiest people are content with what they have. They want little.

I refer to an ancient poem written by a Japanese wise man. He looks at his children who want and need so much in despair. He has become old and now he realises all he needs is his health, family, friends, bed, food and food bowl. Apart from his age, he is happier than he has ever been.

Wanting creates unhappiness because you have a need that you cannot satisfy and as a result you are not as happy **now**.

The more you own the more concerned you become by these possessions. Possessions can entrap you through worry and work. For instance, you collect much jewellery then this causes you to worry about security and insurance. You buy a large house then it needs more maintenance, cleaning and insurance.

The less you want the happier you will be. So picture yourself being content with what you have and not needing anything.

> It is possible to live happily in the here and now. So many conditions of happiness are available -- more than enough for you to be happy right now. You don't have to run into the future in order to get more.
> Thich Nhat Kanh

Right Now I am OK

This is one of my favourite visualisations. In fact, I **always** find it comforting. It is one of the lessons you learn from being mindful. It is the thought that 'right now' I am okay. Right this minute and for a while all is well and I am happy. There is no need to worry about the past or the future. I can live like this. I am not under threat. I don't need unwelcome thoughts. I am healthy and not in pain or feeling unwell. I am free to do what I want. I have a roof over my head. I am doing what I want to do. I have my arms, my legs, sight and hearing. I have snacks at my side. I have a warm cup of tea and so forth. I relax and all thoughts apart from enjoying now fall away.

In times when I worry about the future or reminisce unfavourable about the past, I reach for this thought.

When you visualise the future where you will be a better person constantly say "I will be okay then'. Recall the feeling that you are 'okay right now'. Do you need to think about the future? Do you need to think about the past? Is something going to make you unwell? Is there anything really wrong? All will be okay.

<u>Forever is composed of nows.</u>
<u>Emily Dickinson</u>

Being Assertive

Most people recognise and admire 'nice' people. Nice people are generous, forgive quickly and always understand. What great qualities. Unfortunately, there are many selfish people who are ready to take advantage of anyone who is happy to give them what they need or want. These people can easily sleep at night and their conscience does not bother them. They are often the most charming and endearing people. They have learnt the art of manipulation.

I would be able to live a year with all the money I have lost to needy people. I would not feel so bad aout myself for being such a fool. I would not spend as much time wondering how people can be like this. I would not keep wondering why I lost good friends when all I did was try to help.

Learning to say 'no' is about assertiveness. Many of us have difficulty saying 'no' when asked to do or give something. Of course, being a nice person you won't care because you won't see the abuse. You will give needy people what they want all the time. At the time, you will even feel good about it but later serious issues may arise.

Learn to say 'no'. Sometimes you can do this gently and reapply the pressure. I helped a friend do this recently. My generous loving friend looked after an unknown man's dog for a weekend. It suited her because she liked dogs and did not have one of her own. She did not expect any reward, nor did she get one. Then the man asked if she could look after the dog for a week. She happily accepted but this time expected a reward for her effort. When the man came back he gave her a cheap box of chocolates. Months passed and then the man planned a two-week holiday. Again he approached my friend who became troubled. She felt she was being used. She was upset but would look after the dog anyway. She had been fretting all day. It took much effort to look after the dog. It needed to be walked and fed every day and it prevented her from going out at nights. I recognised her behaviour because I had been the same. She either had to say 'no' or 'here are the terms'. After a discussion the solution was simple. We decided on a simple text saying 'I would be happy to look after your dog but I would need paying', perfectly reasonable. This put the ball in the man's court and perhaps now he felt discomfort. He replied 'That would be fine. How much?' Again my friend felt under pressure. We decided on a fair but cheap price. He happily paid the next day, a week before he left. What was a problem and was causing concern just evaporated with a little action.

When building a visualisation picture yourself saying 'no' to some other people's needs. Picture yourself as your needs coming first and you deserve it. The request might be a favour, someone bullying you into something you don't want to do, lending money and so forth. See yourself having gentle excuses to saying 'no' diplomatically but if it comes to it say and outright 'no'. This is an important part of any visualisation because being assertive earns respect and saves you trouble in the future.

Never feel bad for being assertive, speaking your mind, and putting your foot down. What you think is anger, others see as a good solid display of self-esteem.
Alison James

Lending & Borrowing & Favours

Lending and borrowing money can cause unnecessary problems. A loan to family or a friend is often loose. The payment date and the terms are open ended. Even when the date is agreed because it is between friends or family it is easier for the borrower not to take any agreements seriously. Often, the priority of paying back the money is low. People who borrow money are often willing to pay interest and meet their minimums on their credit cards instead of paying back the full loan. If you are a lender you will start to worry about getting the money back. Even worse, it could grow to irritation. More awkward, the borrower could even ask for more and delay the payment date. Then it can get difficult to refuse or ask for the money back. Then you might not want to see this person.

The result might be that you lose both your money and your friend and fall out with family members. It is far better to never be involved is such arrangements unless you have the money to lose and won't fall out with the borrower.

The same goes for too many favours. If you keep doing favours for people you may find the receiver is never willing to do anything for you. Again this will cause irritation and bad feelings.

See yourself as never lending money to others. See yourself as only providing favours that you don't mind being returned. Never being owed favours or money will bring greater inner-peace.

<u>Neither a borrower nor a lender be,
For loan oft loses both itself and friend,
And borrowing dulls the edge of husbandry.
Hamlet - William Shakespeare</u>

Self-affirmation & Be Proud of Yourself

Unless you are a mass murderer or so forth be proud of yourself and don't care what others think. People see flaws in a person as character. If you are perfect you will probably lack character. As all of us are imperfect we like to see some identifiable blemishes in others.

Without realising we build a negative narrative of our life without reaffirming the positives. We discount our skills, achievements, good feedback from others and focus on the small faults we have and grow them out of proportion. Self-affirmation is about reinforcing the good and not allowing you to get so distracted by other events in your life.

A few lines of my self-affirmation list follow. For a time I wrote down three a day. It helps.

- I am well
- I feel good
- I am not in pain
- I am kind
- I have all my body parts and they work
- I have a roof over my head
- No one has died recently
- I am much better off than many people
- I have a degree

These few self-affirmations far outweigh any negatives I have in my life right now. It amazes me how much I concentrate on what is wrong when so much is right. Imagine of one of the self-affirmations was not true.

<u>Believe you can and you're halfway there.
Theodore Roosevelt</u>

There was a Buddhist monk who spoke about building a large wall. Most of the wall was perfect but a few bricks could have been laid better. When the monk looked at the wall all he saw were the bad bricks. When others looked at the wall they thought it was perfect. We are all like this. We all tend to focus on our bad points and not realise others see no faults and overlook the bad bricks. Also, we have a habit of seeing other people as perfect without realising they have flaws too.

See yourself being proud of yourself regardless of any faults. See yourself as appreciating all that you have. Remind yourself and focus on all your good points. Build on the good.

<u>Self-criticism and negative thoughts about yourself will attract people who reflect this back to you, showing critical behaviour and can abuse you physically.</u>

<u>Hina Hashmi</u>

Smile

How attractive do you find people who fittingly smile much of the time?

How hard is it to be angry or confrontational with a smiling person?

> I've never seen a smiling face that was not beautiful.
> Author unknown

When you smile or laugh the brain releases 'good feeling' chemicals. These chemicals are even released when you are not fully smiling.

There are many benefits of smiling. Smiling reduces the heart rate, stress, encourages people to be empathetic with you, is contagious, builds trust, increases life expectancy, boosts the immune system and so forth.

See yourself smiling and laughing more as you pass through life. Think of happy memories and visualise your favourite people and places. Remember your happy smiles and bring them back. Be open to enjoy other people's smiles and laughter. People enjoy the company of smiling people and think them attractive. Acting happy will make you happier.

> The world always looks brighter from behind a smile.
> Author unknown

Explore Solutions

In life, you often need to solve social problems. The only issue is that some people turn to the same fixes over and again even though they are not the best fit. You need to watch out for predetermined solutions and question them. For instance, your normal fix if someone upset you might be to avoid them. Is this the only solution? Is this the best solution? A better solution might be to talk.

It is important to examine whether your natural solutions to problems are the best. Sometimes, coming up with solutions on your own is difficult. I recommend that you discuss events and potential fixes with other people who may have better ideas.

<u>One cannot conquer alone.</u>
<u>Translated Russian Saying</u>

First seek the best fix either by thinking out of the box or by discussion. Then visualise yourself carrying out the steps needed to use the solution.

<u>A fault confessed is half redressed.</u>
<u>Translated Russian Saying</u>

Do Your Best & Acceptance

I find this a comforting thought because it is true and takes away responsibility for trying to achieve more. You can only do your best. If your best is not good enough well you just have to accept that. It is easy to accept and move on if you tried your best.

<u>A man can do no more than he can.</u>
<u>Chinese saying</u>

At my age, I will never be able to run one hundred metres in less than ten seconds. Is there any point in continually wishing I could? I could do my best and run one hundred meters in sixteen seconds I simply have to accept that.

See yourself always doing the best you can. You cannot let yourself down if you do. Visualise yourself **accepting** your limitations and do not make the error of beating yourself up for the impossible.

Help Others & Giving

> Doing nothing for others is the undoing of ourselves.
> Horace Mann

I feel nothing gives me more satisfaction these days than giving. If I have no worth then at least let me give. I then have worth. It makes me happier and lessens the problems I think I have. Giving often leads to recognising that others are going through a rough time too. Even when you give without receiving it somehow comes back. The people you help may be strangers, family, friends, colleagues or neighbours. Volunteering, giving your time, caring, helping, giving gifts and so forth all bring happiness to you and others.

Picture yourself giving without expecting anything back and your soul will feel cleansed.

> For it is in giving that we receive.
> Francis of Assisi

Be Truthful & Honest

<u>A clear conscience is a soft pillow.</u>
<u>German Proverb</u>

It is hard work lying and remembering your lies. Occasionally you will trip up and just look bad. Even worse people spot your lies and mistrust you or lose respect. You have no guilt when you don't deceive or lie. Honesty has a calming and peaceful effect and everybody knows who you are.

Picture yourself as truthful and honest because you know deceit brings no good.

<u>A liar should be a person of good memory.</u>
<u>Translated Russian Saying</u>

Be Humble

You might be bounding with self-esteem and that is good. You might be better than most around you and have much ability. Maybe you are overbearingly filled with pride. If you are bragging at all you are not living as a humble person.

What is humble? Humble is not over-evaluating yourself above others. It is about recognising the talents and qualities of other people. It is accepting you have limits. It is about respecting others. It is about not putting people down. It is not about competing with others to be better or be the best.

If you are to compete with anyone compete with yourself. Concentrate on improving yourself, reaching your own goals and new levels where other people are do not matter. Defer their criticism and opinions of you. They may be true but listen, accept and move on with confidence.

<u>Don't teach fish to swim.
Translated Russian Saying</u>

<u>A boaster and a liar are first cousins.
Translated Russian Saying</u>

People around you have much wisdom and if you open yourself you may grow and gather good advice. You might have a view that meditation is for people wearing tie-dye shirts, baggy trousers who smoke marijuana. You might think meditation will never work for you. Be open and try it a few times before you close the door. I opened many doors when I changed my view to try it first and then decide if it has any value for me.

People value humble people as they feel comfortable and respected. Picture yourself as quieter, humble, no better than anyone else. Listen and learn.

<u>We learn something from everyone who passes through our lives.. Some lessons are painful, some are painless and some are priceless.</u>
<u>Unknown</u>

Empathy & Walk In Their Shoes

Empathy is wonderful. Handing out empathy makes people respect and like you. They realise that you understand them. Remember how you felt when people understood why you did something, how you felt and so on. Remember how angry you were when someone criticised you without understanding. When you understand someone it is harder to be angry with them.

Picture yourself having the time to empathise with people more. See yourself as walking in their shoes.

<u>Before you criticise a man, walk a mile in his shoes.
Based on American Indian saying</u>

Accept Your Shadow

People often say 'I did this but it is not me'. Consider this as your shadow. If we are honest we do some things a lot but put them away in the 'that is not me' category. This is simply rejecting yourself. There is much discomfort by not embracing your full self. There is a part of you that does not fit into your values and beliefs. It is an uncomfortable contradiction. You fight it. It is hard work. It is far better to say 'that is me now and again I would prefer to change it'.

See yourself as embracing all of yourself even the bad parts.

<u>The most terrifying thing is to accept oneself completely.</u>
C. J. Jung

Addiction & Habits

Addiction is a problem to feel that lovely reward or hide problems despite the unfavourable consequences. Some people have more susceptibility because of their genes. Addiction, almost by definition, is hard to overcome.

If you have an addiction to heroin, cocaine, gambling, smoking, shopping and so forth you probably need to get professional help. Most people cannot overcome addiction on their own. Chemical addiction can need medical care.

It is not in the scope of this book to address addiction specifically but some can be dealt with like bad habits or at least part of them can.

We may have bad habits which are not good for us. Visualisation can be good for overcoming these habits. However, there is no point just simply seeing yourself as eating less, not biting your nails and so forth and hoping it will happen. Further visualisation is needed on the bad effects of the habit and the benefits of overcoming it.

This is best illustrated by example. You want to give up biting your nails.

First, see yourself as a person that does not bite their nails.

Second, picture the bad. For instance, the grimy dirt and germs you consume. Feel the pain of the occasional infection you get. See how disgusting your nails look when people see them and so forth.

Finally, see the good. For instance, see yourself confidently reaching for a mug and not feeling self-conscious of your fingers. See yourself feeling better and so on.

A change in bad habits leads to a change in life.
Jenny Craig

You Can Only Control So Much

There are many people I know that want total control of every aspect of their lives. This is unrealistic and is a huge mental drain. So much so, that it significantly harms enjoyment of the moment. To control most events you will continually fail and this will create unnecessary ill feelings. Control often leads to the need for perfection too. To achieve perfection can be an unreasonable goal. Sure, perfection at times may be necessary or desirable. However, often achieving perfection is unnecessary. Besides, sometimes achieving perfection is simply impossible.

With mental health, I dislike the word 'control'. Control needs much effort and failure is a possibility. I prefer words like 'manage'. The word 'manage' implies when events occur that you cannot control you deal with them.

We have little control over most events or conditions. 'Control' is so much of an issue that in Alcoholics Anonymous Twelve Steps, the first is as follows:

> God grant me the serenity to accept the things I cannot change, the courage to change the things I can, and the wisdom to know the difference.
> Reinhold Niebuhr

This is important. There is simply no point in spending time worrying about what you cannot control. Perhaps, you are short and hate it. Unfortunately, there is nothing you can do about this apart from accepting it.

See yourself letting go of all circumstances you cannot control. Picture yourself as free of everything that you simply have to accept. Never picture trying to control what you cannot.

Acceptance will bring much inner peace.

Forgive Yourself

Forgiving yourself is one of the most important paths to internal freedom. You are like everyone else. We make mistakes. We have flaws. We regret how we behaved in certain situations. Forgive yourself. Perhaps you were mentally unwell, suffering from PMS, angry at something, might have an addiction, were drunk, need to address the way you think, don't know or so on. If the people you impacted had anything about them they should understand. If they don't they should as they themselves have their own problems. It is their responsibility. Forgive yourself as you would a friend or a loved one. You know you are not bad and you have simply slipped. You will probably see others make mistakes and they should not cause deep pain. Nor should you about your own failings. It makes you human.

> The weak can never forgive. Forgiveness is the attribute of the strong.
> Mahatma Gandhi

'Don't be so hard on yourself' is another way of forgiveness. There is no doubt we are our own worst enemies. We often easily forgive others for actions that we have done ourselves. We have such high expectations of ourselves but not so much for others. Why? How does that benefit you? Whatever we have done there were positives. You have learnt, you have grown, you are more skilled and are less likely to make the mistake again. You might positively change the way you address the future. The worse the experience often results in the greatest future gain.

<u>Do not look where you fell, but where you slipped.
African proverb</u>

Don't put yourself down. There are enough people who will do that for you. There is an inner voice that says 'I shouldn't', 'I can't', 'I am strange, 'I am slow', 'I am not as good as other people', 'I always mess up' and so forth. It is best to replace this inner voice with much more positive messages. You are not fooling yourself because these positive thoughts are true. Instead, think 'I could have', 'I can', 'Everyone has unwanted traits and so do I, that is what makes me beautiful', 'We are all slow at some things', 'everyone messes up', and so on. Others make mistakes and have weaknesses too. Other people's mistakes might not be the same as yours but you can be sure they battle with their inner voice too.

So there are some people who have not forgiven you. If they knew you and cared they should have. Have they seen your good points? Do they know your history? Do they know about your unique problems? Are they denying their own issues? Their own problems might be more understandable and acceptable to others but how can they judge you. Why do they think your problem is worse than theirs? If they reflected and had true empathy and understanding they would know. Their inability to empathise is simply their weakness, not yours. Do not own the whole problem.

If they are not willing to get to know you further there is only one choice. Let these people go. Stop caring about what they think. Don't worry about meeting them again. Don't let their negativity influence your life.

<u>He is not wise that is not wise for himself.
English Proverb</u>

Picture yourself as good but not infallible. Accept you slip now and again. See others as fallible too. See yourself as forgiven for all the events in the past. After all the past is gone and all you can deal with is now and the future. See yourself as good as any other person. Always visualise yourself without the errors of the past. Picture yourself doing better in the future.

Forgive Others & Let go of Anger & Hate

You have to decide when another's behaviour to you will become a 'breaker'. It is best to do this when you are not thinking about a particular person or situation and develop a policy. If something has recently happened be honest with yourself. Does this person deserve forgiveness? If the person has repeated their behaviour it may be too much of an insult. If they don't deserve forgiveness then I suggest that you cut them out of your life. There are many people in this world who deserve your attention and will not take advantage of you. Also, it is important to remove all excessively negative people from your life if you can.

Forgiving people who have wronged or harmed you will bring you much relief. It is a burden to carry any negative feelings to others. In some ways, you hurt yourself twice. Also, you are holding on to the past.

> Darkness cannot drive out darkness; only light can do that. Hate cannot drive out hate; only love can do that.
> Martin Luther King, Jr

Comments from other people can hurt. It is interesting that if these comments don't touch some truth or belief they rarely hurt. For instance, now if someone called me fat it does not hurt as I know it is the truth. Ten years before, if someone had called me overweight it would crush me because I had not accepted the truth. There is some insensitivity in the person who said I was fat but I no longer care. I now understand that if something hurts me I have to be honest and ask why. This is more often than not their problem not mine. Some things you can address the others you simply have to accept.

<u>None can hurt me without my permission.
Gandhi</u>

Unpleasant people have issues and are in pain themselves. They often reveal it with undesirable comments. Putting other people down gives them comfort. It does not make sense for a person to hurt you for no reason. Always view the event as not being your issue but theirs. This is assuming that there was nothing you did to bring it on yourself. You probably already know that when you were disagreeable your nastiness may have been misplaced and it was more your own issue. It was some pain or anguish that came out of you. You may have misperceived the situation. Reflect on this, as your nastiness was ill-directed and imbalanced. That may be true of a nasty person too.

<u>Deal with the faults of others as gently as with your own.
Chinese Proverb</u>

Is a person that judges quickly and harshly without knowing you worth anything? Why think to yourself that you are worthless and laden with faults. Even though you might want to impress this person and want them to like you they are shallow. So why do you care what they think?

<u>Anger can be an expensive luxury.
Italian Proverb</u>

Anger is a great motivator for change. It often causes us to talk to someone and understand what is bothering us. Expressing anger is sometimes good and helps release unwanted emotions. However, we know people who have outbursts of anger and especially if it is prolonged can harm people. Some people need specialist help to control and manage anger.

> You will not be punished for your anger, you will be punished by your anger.
> Buddha

Many of us have learnt not to show or express outrage. Anger is often considered taboo. No doubt at points in your life you have not expressed your annoyance because you were not allowed. For example, a teacher may have chastised you by mistake. You have no choice in our society but to conceal your fury.

Constantly dwelling on something or someone you are angry with is unhealthy. Carrying hate or anger normally only damages the holder.

> Anger is an acid that can do more harm to the vessel in which it is stored than to anything on which it is poured.
> Mark Twain

See yourself as being free of all anger, irritation and hate. See yourself as resolving problems without bad emotions and through discussion rather than argument. Picture yourself as seeing the good in everyone. See yourself as letting go of bad emotions directed to others. Picture the relief as you remove negative people from your life.

Letting Go & Drop Burdens

What is letting go? Letting go is not about 'getting rid' of thoughts and feelings about the past and the future. It is about sensibly detaching from them and not allowing them to ruin the current moment.

Time passes. The older you get the more the past weighs down. So do thoughts about the future as you gain responsibilities. It is like you are carrying a slowly filling rucksack with heavy rocks. The weight of the rucksack hinders your enjoyment of this moment and that is all that matters.

The past is gone and cannot be relived. Little needs to be planned in the future. So how do you free yourself from these unnecessary burdens? If you were going on a long hike wouldn't you just like to open the rucksack and drop all the rocks? Like dropping the rocks, there is no reason you can't let your mind free and concentrate on now.

Close your eyes. Identify the events that concern you about the past and the future, imagine throwing them out of the rucksack. Also imagine each major and worrying thought as a rock and throw that out too. Feel your rucksack become lighter until it is empty. Picture yourself as always carrying an empty rucksack and emptying any weight as soon as you can. The past and future are unnecessary burdens so see yourself freeing yourself from them.

I don't carry the burden of the past or the madness of the future. I live in the present.
Narendra Modi

Risk & Pain

Living involves risk and pain.

There are risks we cannot avoid. Every day we drive we risk an accident. Every day we live we risk disease. There is even danger in living in a house. All we can do is accept this. In many religions there is a saying 'it is god's will'.

Pain is something we experience at some time. It is part of life. Avoiding any future pain would lessen the full enjoyment of life. It is better to handle and manage the emotional pain and feel.

> The pain you feel today is the strength you feel tomorrow. For every challenge faced there is opportunity for growth.
> Unknown

I remember talking to the sister-in-law of my x-wife, Eve. She had the greatest misfortune and lost her child at eighteen months because she drowned in a bath. Later, I was in the presence of someone who asked a brave question. They asked Eve if she would have preferred to have never had the child. She replied 'I am so grateful for the time I had with her' and it was far better to have met her even though the pain of the loss is so great. I remember this as it changed my attitude to life. There is no point letting the risk of losing something preventing you experiencing it. In fact, some of the best experiences come from risk.

<u>T'is better to have loved and than to have never loved at all.
Alfred Lord Tennyson</u>

Picture yourself simply accepting that risk and pain are life. Everyone suffers pain at some time. See yourself accepting pain when it comes as normal. See pain as having positives on your self-development.

Write It Down

There are three good reasons for writing thoughts down. First, to throw away or release yourself from any worries you have. Second, to focus on what matters. Finally, to clear your mind as much as possible.

The most important reason to write concerning thoughts down is to free yourself as much as possible from thoughts that are weighing you down and running wild. When you are having difficulty getting to sleep and repetitively worrying it is best to reach peace by writing the concerns down and then throwing them away. Somehow writing them down decreases the power of the issues and allows you to focus on resolving them. Writing all your issues down lessens your problems as it puts everything into perspective.

Often we get so caught up with being busy with everyday events we lose focus on what matters to us. It is important to keep focus on the big issues, not the small ones. Sometimes, I think people have a 'worry bucket' and it always has to be full. So even when there is nothing significant to worry about the bucket becomes full of small worries when there is no need.

Sometimes, writing issues down helps you focus on overcoming a life problem. For example, my girlfriend dumped me after a long relationship. Of course, that was very painful. Like many other people I got relief from listing down her bad points. By continually reviewing these bad points it showed me the relationship was not good anyway.

See yourself replacing all the worries on your list for the sake of the big picture. The problems are often not as powerful as you think. See yourself writing down thoughts that keep occupying your mind. Once written, see yourself letting go of them.

<u>Worry often gives a small thing a big shadow.
Swedish Proverb</u>

Time Heals

They say 'time heals all wounds'. Unfortunately, it doesn't but it does heal many.

One of the most painful experiences I have had was when I broke up with a partner. For a long time, I could not believe life would ever be 'normal' and pain-free again. However, time has passed and I am glad we broke up. The wound has healed and time was a major factor.

For a moment, think about how many things in the past were painful but after time they lost their 'hurt'. Indeed, there are so many of them that you have forgotten most. You can overcome your current wounds in time even though one day they may leave a scar.

See yourself as getting over all worries in time. See that worries will pass so there is no reason to forget them immediately and to hold onto them. Most bad feelings will go in time, so will this one.

> The two most powerful warriors are patience and time.
> Leo Tolstoy

Learn From Mistakes

You have made mistakes, you have failed. Settle yourself to moving on. The past is gone. Mistakes are soon forgotten by most but you. Resolve yourself to start anew. You will not make the mistake again, or at least not as easily. Address how you will improve yourself and then do it. It is time to forget the past and move on. There is nothing more you can do so relax.

> The only man who never makes a mistake is the man who never does anything.
> Theodore Roosevelt

See yourself learning from every mistake you make. See yourself making the improvements you identified that led to the mistake. Picture yourself proud of the lesson you learnt. See yourself with lack of regret as everyone makes mistakes. Picture yourself as stronger and better having made the mistake because you have developed.

> Learn from past mistakes to avoid future ones.
> Chinese saying

Body Language

Most of our communication is non-verbal. Twenty to thirty percent of our communication comes from tone of voice, facial expressions, gestures, eye-contact, head movements, hand movements and so on. There is a wide range of features that contribute to body language.

If you adopt suitable body language your mind will follow. It is not possible to manage all body language as it secretly reveals your inner feelings and how you see yourself. However, over time as you feel better your body language will follow.

As you visualise show your body language suitably fitting the pictures you have built. How you see yourself performing better.

> Body language is a very powerful tool. We had body language before we had speech, and apparently, 80% of what you understand in a conversation is read through the body, not the words.
> Deborah Bull

Arguments & Less Emotion

Like a mirror what you say is only a reflection of yourself. If you find yourself having negative conversations or sharing viscous opinions, think to yourself what am I saying about myself.

See yourself taking out emotions from discussions to avoid arguments and convey a stronger self. Picture yourself under control and calm.

<u>Those who in quarrels interpose, must often wipe a bloody nose.
Translated Russian Saying</u>

VISUALISATIONS TO AVOID CHECKLIST

The following sections include general themes that you must avoid in your visualisations as they will be counterproductive. You should use this as a checklist to make sure you do not include any of these bad thoughts.

Texting & Impulse Communication

Texting, emailing and posting on social networks is a problem for some people. Some people have an urge to communicate, reassure themselves or resolve difficulties using social sites or texting. Sometimes when we have had a few drinks we don't judge what we are saying and why we say it. Our view can be poor and we can read more unintended meaning into other people's messages and posts. We can even start to place importance on the time the person has taken to reply.

Text and social messages can easily be misread and misunderstood. Sometimes you can even type a word you didn't mean. For instance, you might have wanted to say 'I was glad to meet you' yet you said 'I was sad to meet you'. This is not only when you send messages but when you receive them. There is no body language, smiling, facial expression, voice tone, seeing how the other person reacts and so forth. It is said that only 7% of full communication occurs with a text versus face-to-face contact. Can you have clear communication only using 7% of your expressive potential? So use texting for light communication. Some messages or posts may lead to regret, shame, even embarrassment and is a permanent record.

Messaging, texting and posting can cause relationship problems and are not the best method for resolving sensitive issues or arguments. The problem can be self-perpetuating. Each message can lead to further actions and damage. Self-esteem, self-confidence and self-worth can all decrease regardless of the relationship damage.

Think to yourself would it not be better to call or meet face-to-face? If you feel uncomfortable calling or meeting doesn't this mean your relationship is rocky or you don't know the person well enough? It suggests electronic communication is inappropriate.

Visualise that you never do anything on impulse and you will wait a day until you send a message. See yourself not repeatedly following up texts because you did not get the answer you wanted. See yourself never discussing sensitive and vulnerable subjects electronically.

Avoid resolving important issues using social media or messaging. Avoid revealing vulnerable emotions. No texting, messaging and posting can make you feel more peaceful.

> ... every impulse of feeling should be guided by reason.
> Jane Austen

Over Thinking The Future

I watched a video made by a Buddhist monk called Ajahn Brahm. He said he could predict Australia's future for the next ten years with 100 per cent accuracy. The audience paused in disbelief. The monk then paused for effect. Then he said, "it is uncertain!" He smiled. Isn't that so true? Isn't that all you can say about the future?

<u>Coming events cast their shadows before them</u>
<u>Chinese Saying</u>

There is some of the future you can predict with some certainty. You may know that tomorrow you need to take the children to school. In a few days, you need to pay the electricity bill. On Friday you may have a weekly meeting at work. But even these may not happen. An event may occur, like the school closes for a day, you win a large sum of money, you have an accident and so forth.

Some of this future you do need to think about. For example, I must pay the energy bill else there will be no electricity. Some of your effort does need to plan. You may need to have the car fixed soon to take the children to school. With all these tasks and events you just need a plan. Then there is no point in worrying about them until they need to be done.

Thinking that you will never meet anyone, you will never be happy again, the person tomorrow will confront me, nothing will happen next week and so on is a waste of energy. Can you remember when you accurately predicted the future before and when you got a few nice surprises? I doubt it. Avoid over-thinking and trying to predict the future especially based on the past.

<u>The foolish man seeks happiness in the distance,
the wise grows it under his feet.
Translated Russian Saying</u>

Saying Sorry Too Much

Some people say sorry for nearly everything. This is an irritating quality. It is a sign the person is overly worried about offending people and shows lack of confidence.

Avoid saying sorry often and reserve apologies to important matters. Apologies must be genuine and a person who apologises for everything loses the power to provide a 'real' apology. A genuine apology is powerful, needs strength, repairs relationships, brings about forgiveness and so forth.

<u>A man is sorry to be honest for nothing.</u>
<u>Ovid</u>

Procrastination

What is procrastination? It is putting off or postponing actions you would like to take. Avoid procrastination and make sure it is not part of any visualisation.

Some people suffer from procrastination and some consider it to be the act of ruining your life for no obvious reason. There are people who talk good plans but never get around to taking the necessary action. For some people, procrastination is an inner struggle and causes much discomfort. It makes them unhappy, causes regrets and lowers self-esteem. Sometimes procrastination is a worse problem than people realise. Are you one of those people who leave a 'must do' task to the last-minute? Worse, you spent much time worrying about doing it?

The obvious answer would be to start doing. The problem is that procrastinators fear the word 'do' and know they are not going to get instant gratification. As a result, some may consider procrastination a selfish act.

So what can you do? You are a good planner so break the task into little pieces. Aim to just improve and reward yourself for improvement. Aim for slow steady progress. Remember this book has been written one sentence at a time. The most important step is to start the first piece as soon as possible. Commit to a time or schedule, even if for small chunks of time. Try to do as much as you can. Always come back to the task and only commit yourself to a little task. When visualising see yourself doing each step. Visualise how good you will feel as you complete each step. Visualise enjoying doing and not some horrific task. See yourself relaxing, getting a cup of tea, setting up a comfortable environment, putting on the radio and so forth. Concentrate on the end goal and the satisfaction you will get when you reach it. Try to consider the alternative entertainment as boring but enjoyed more after success.

If you procrastinate, at least you bought this book. Well done on at least doing that. You have decided you need to change so now the challenge is to put the book into action.

Putting something off provides bad feelings. Doing provides good feelings. If you are going to continue to put actions off it is better not to commit yourself to them in the first place.

Greater inner-peace awaits those who start doing and feeling good about themselves.

> <u>My advice is to never do tomorrow what you can do today. Procrastination is the thief of time.</u>
> <u>Charles Dickens</u>

Impulse Buying

Impulse buying leads to regret and later financial issues. It is a means of providing excitement about the future and then instant gratification. It can be an addiction. The indulgence is rarely worth the later regret or bad feelings.

You could foresee the damage impulse buying does and fully recognise how bad it is. You could see the instant gratification is so short and not as great. However, avoiding impulse buying is beyond the bounds of this book. Avoid visualising anything to do with instant gratification that you know is not for the long-term good. Impulse buying is counterproductive to the objectives of this book.

> We all nurture impulses which promise freedom from the demands of others, even if that freedom means death.
> Sam Tanenhaus

Judging & Self Reflection

How much time do you spend judging others? By judging, I mean picking out the negative qualities of another person. How often have you joined in a negative chat about someone and your real aim is to bond with the other people judging? If you do have negative feelings about someone else what does that say about you? It is natural to judge. We may inwardly think that a person's hairstyle doesn't look good, that person angers easily and so forth. Some of these judgements are useful, if you see someone who angers easily you may tread more carefully.

You are responsible for getting your judgements right especially when they have no benefit to you. Some people judge other people so much they create inner unhappiness. The happier you are in yourself the less likely your need to judge others. Most judgement is a reflection of yourself. Often the person you judge does not know so the only person that can get hurt is you. You are negatively attacking yourself and trying to put someone else down. Judgement comes with a lack of security in ourselves, fear of non-acceptance from others and so forth. Judgement makes you feel worse in yourself, hurts other people, tries to remove individuals and make the stereotypes that comfort you and encourages negative self-judgement. Remember you want to be yourself and not someone else.

How do you deal with judgement? See yourself as accepting other people as they are. Why judge them? What does it do for you? See yourself as not wanting to be a stereotype. See yourself focusing on yourself and not others. Remember how you felt when you have found people highlighting your negatives. Do you want to hurt other people in this way? Look for people's positives not negatives as you would like to do for yourself. Allow and want individuals in your life. Individuality is the spice of life and none of us are stereotypes. Don't hurt people and hurt yourself by feeling bad or guilty. See yourself accepting and being happy with yourself.

Avoid judging others and certainly do not include any judgements into your visualisations.

<u>How easy it is to judge rightly after one sees what evil comes from judging wrongly!
Elizabeth Gaskell</u>

Rushing

We have a tendency to rush around, possibly in a disorganised way and let life pass without enjoyment. Many of us could reflect on the past and wonder where life has gone. Mindfulness is about enjoying the moment and rushing is harmful. Avoid visualising yourself rushing through tasks or through the visualisation. In doing this you are encouraging behaviour you do not want.

> Nature never rushes, yet everything gets done
> Donald Hicks

Being the Victim

Are you always the victim? Some people who always play the victim often don't think they are. They fall out with their friends, have relationship problems, forever are in a crisis and so forth. They never play a part in these events. They hurt and spend much of their time unhappy. Victims always think that someone else is to blame for nearly all the avoidable bad that happens. They also constantly complain to people around them that life is not going well and look for sympathy, self-affirmation and agreement that nothing is their fault. You may have friends on Facebook you will see a few victims. They are the ones who constantly post bad news and have to tell you about it. Their thoughts are so negative they don't have any gratitude for the good surrounding them. Their life is always worse than anybody else's as bad luck always follows them. They are always looking for attention, hugs and kisses. Eventually, victims leave a bad taste in your mouth. I believe the core issue is a lack of self-esteem and fear to take responsibility for their own lives.

See yourself not thinking like a victim and being responsible for all ambitions, relationships and achievements. Realise that change is up to you and no one else. See yourself as not needing attention from others to feel better. Picture yourself responding more positively to events you could have influenced. See yourself as taking the risks even when there is potential failure or rejection. See yourself saying 'I can' and 'I will' rather than 'I can't' and 'I won't'. When you stop feeling the victim it is likely there will be an empty void. Now you have to take responsibility and to go without continual approval from others. Picture yourself as being okay not being the victim. See that being the victim attracts negative views and you will be a better person. By not being the victim you benefit many times over.

Negative Self-talk

Self-talk reveals what you think and how you see yourself. Negative self-talk means that you are not thinking positively about yourself and you know this has to change. Positive self-talk is part of changing to a better person and is the way you could be thinking.

Do not visualise any negative self-talk rather change to positive and uplifting self-talk. Starting to talk to yourself positively will assist the changes that you want to make. Avoid picturing yourself saying 'I should', 'I can't' and replace them with words like 'I could', 'I can' and so on.

> Your subconscious mind is always listening to and believing in everything you repeatedly say about yourself. So try not to become your own enemy of progress.
> Edmond Mbiaka

Jealousy

Jealousy can be a nasty emotion. We think everyone else is having a great time and we are missing something. It is complex and combines many feelings from fear, abandonment, comparison, judgement, shame, rage and humiliation. Jealousy might be apt sometimes perhaps when you are a child to make sure you are not ignored. A little jealousy experienced over a short time is normal and perhaps suggests what you want. However, in general, jealousy is a feeling that does more harm than good. I see people suffering from jealousy for a wide range of reasons. Fortunately, some understanding can relieve much of this unpleasant and gripping emotion. The realisation that jealousy is an issue is the first step to resolution.

<u>A competent and self-confident person is incapable of jealousy in anything. Jealousy is invariably a symptom of neurotic insecurity.</u>
Robert A. Heinlein

The first reason we often get jealous is that we compare. What has that person got that I cannot? Why was that woman born so beautiful and gets all the attention and I do not? How did I lose my girlfriend to that guy? Without comparisons and want, there is no jealousy. How often do we get jealous of one quality a person has or event and lose sight of the whole picture? It is just one comparison. The person you are jealous of have their own inadequacies and problems. Of course, you may experience disappointment but that is a lesser emotion.

The second common theme is inadequacy, lack of self-esteem and lack of value. These are all feelings in you. They can cause incorrect emotions like jealousy because you become needy.

Thirdly, jealousy can come from how the world is perceived, what you think of yourself and how you imagine the perfect world should be. Pain can come from wanting to fit in with your perceived world.

See yourself shifting your view and not comparing yourself to others. Picture yourself accepting that you cannot always get what you want. No one can.

You can't always get what you want.
English Proverb

Being Someone Else

One of the biggest regrets people have when they are dying is they were not themselves. They found it difficult to reveal their true selves and express their feelings. They were living as someone else. If you are by nature protective, quiet and closed and so on it is fine. Trying to be an extrovert and open is not you. To have a unique personality is endearing. You will strengthen some relationships and be able to talk about your past and more likely to be liked and get empathy.

>If people reach perfection they vanish, you know.
>T.H. White

Be yourself and give up trying to be different or like someone else. Being someone else or your ideal image of what you want to be is hard work. Being yourself is fulfilling. You may end up fighting yourself, in internal turmoil and disappointed. What is the problem of being yourself? People respect individuals. They respect people who are confident of themselves. We have sides that we do not want to reveal. There is no problem.

Slowly build yourself to tell your partner what you want. Tell them what you like and what you don't. Share yourself. You will be surprised.

Tell people what you think. If you are talking about them do it delicately unless it is praise. Praise is excellent.

>Put silk on a goat, and it's still a goat.
>Irish Proverb

Picture yourself as being you, behaving as you feel right, saying what you feel necessary, being proud of who you are and so on. Avoid visualising being different from your true self and behaving like someone else.

Over Caring What People Think

No matter who you are this is true. Some people will hate or dislike you. Some people will love you. Most people won't care. Most people spend most of their time thinking about themselves.

The only way to be is yourself and any forced change because what others think is not right. Let people choose how they want to feel and don't worry. You cannot force people. It is just a shame that more don't love you but that is the way of the world.

> Care about what other people think and you will always be their prisoner.
> Lao Tzu

It doesn't matter what people think if you respect and love yourself. Think of that time when someone deeply loved you and you loved them back. What mattered? Everything was okay. You didn't care then what people think.

> Ultimately what we really are matters more than other people think of us.
> Jawaharlal Nehru

Do not imagine what people might think. This is not part of a picture that you want to concentrate on as it has no benefit.

ISSUES & BASIC VISUALISATIONS CHECKLIST

This chapter contains some basic problems people experience and a guide to visualisations. Remember it is the processes of getting to your goals that are important. Also, you have to use your imagination to address your own needs.

When it is obvious that the goals cannot be reached, don't adjust the goals, adjust the action steps.
Confucius

Unhappy, Unwell, Anxious and Depressed

* PLEASE OBTAIN MEDICAL ASSISTANCE IF MUCH OF BELOW APPLIES *

You see yourself as..

- Uncomfortable anxious all the time.
- Lacking the energy to do things you used to enjoy and have lost interest.
- Generally not feeling physically unwell much of the time - like headaches, aching muscles and malaise.
- Struggling to get up and do anything.
- Mentally uncomfortable and not how you

See yourself as..

- Booking an appointment today.
- Attending the appointment.
- Carrying out the recommendations.

used to be.
- Not being able to concentrate.
- Having difficulty remembering and making decisions.
- Feeling irritable, agitated, sad, hopeless, pessimistic, guilty or shameful.
- Thinking of suicide and death.
- Not being able to sleep or relax.

Self-esteem, Self-worth, Self-respect

You see yourself as..	Visualisation - See yourself as..
<ul><li>Having no self-worth.</li><li>Being nervous and shy.</li><li>Having no self-respect.</li><li>Being embarrassed by much of what you say or your behaviour.</li></ul>	<ul><li>With all those self-affirmations you can write down. Like I am a kind person, I am loyal, I am honest and so forth.</li><li>Positive, calm, assertive.</li><li>Everything I say has value.</li></ul>

SEE RELATED TOPICS

Right Now I am OK
Being Assertive
Self-affirmation & Be Proud of Yourself
Smile
Do Your Best & Acceptance
Be Truthful & Honest
Be Humble
Accept Your Shadow
You Can Only Control So Much
Forgive Yourself

Write It Down
Body Language
Arguments & Less Emotion
Over Thinking The Future
Saying Sorry Too Much
Judging & Self Reflection
Being the Victim
Negative Self-talk
Being Someone Else
Over Caring What People Think

Lack of Companionship and Good Relations

You see yourself as..	Visualisation - See yourself as..
<ul><li>Having no friends or poor relationship with friends.</li><li>With difficulties to get on with people or be liked.</li><li>With difficulties relating to your children and thinking you are a bad parent.</li><li>Never finding a partner.</li><li>Not wanting anyone to see the "real you" because they won't like you.</li></ul>	<ul><li>Being a better friend.</li><li>Realising these are your feelings and there is no real connection and you are responsible for how you feel</li><li>Free of anger.</li><li>Not having any negative self-talk.</li><li>Not procrastinating but taking action and going out and doing things.</li><li>Soft, affectionate, understanding and fun.</li><li>Happy and smile.</li><li>Right now all is okay, so try to not think or</li></ul>

- Being in an unsatisfactory relationship that will never change.
- conjure up the future.
- Having increased sexuality and adventure.
- Changing. Perhaps you need to end the relationship and face all the fears as this will pay in the long-term.
- Becoming the 'parent' and stopping being the child to overcome irritation and dominance from parents.

SEE RELATED TOPICS

What Makes Happy People
Right Now I am OK
Lending & Borrowing & Favours
Self-affirmation & Be Proud of Yourself
Smile
Explore Solutions
Do Your Best & Acceptance
Help Others & Giving
Be Truthful & Honest

- Be Humble
- Empathy & Walk In Their Shoes
- You Can Only Control So Much
- Forgive Yourself
- Forgive Others & Let go of Anger & Hate
- Risk & Pain
- Write It Down
- Learn From Mistakes
- Body Language
- Arguments & Less Emotion
- Texting & Impulse Communication
- Judging & Self Reflection
- Being the Victim
- Negative Self-talk
- Being Someone Else
- Over Caring What People Think

Bad Friends and Negative People

You see yourself as..	Visualisation - See yourself as..
• Being dragged down by some people in your life. Worse you have not realised this is happening yet.	• Taking responsibility for your life. • Slowly dropping negative people from your life and being better without them. They can be replaced by better people in time. • Only letting people affect you if you let them. • Smiling, welcoming and getting on with people you don't get on with and see them as friendly.

SEE RELATED TOPICS

Right Now I am OK
Being Assertive
Lending & Borrowing & Favours
Self-affirmation & Be Proud of Yourself
Smile
Explore Solutions
Do Your Best & Acceptance
Help Others & Giving
Be Truthful & Honest
Be Humble
Empathy & Walk In Their Shoes
You Can Only Control So Much
Forgive Others & Let go of Anger & Hate
Letting Go & Drop Burdens
Risk & Pain
Arguments & Less Emotion
Texting & Impulse Communication
Judging & Self Reflection
Being the Victim
Negative Self-talk
Being Someone Else
Over Caring What People Think

Shame and Guilt

You see yourself as..	Visualisation - See yourself as..
- As carrying a dirty feeling of shame and guilt much of the time.	- Gently and calmly apologising to anyone you have harmed. - Forgive yourself. - Stopping to drink so much alcohol.

SEE RELATED TOPICS

Right Now I am OK
Being Assertive
Lending & Borrowing & Favours
Self-affirmation & Be Proud of Yourself
Do Your Best & Acceptance
Help Others & Giving
Be Truthful & Honest
Be Humble
Empathy & Walk In Their Shoes
Accept Your Shadow
You Can Only Control So Much
Forgive Yourself
Forgive Others & Let go of Anger & Hate
Letting Go & Drop Burdens
Time Heals
Arguments & Less Emotion

Texting & Impulse Communication
Saying Sorry Too Much
Judging & Self Reflection
Being the Victim
Negative Self-talk
Jealousy
Being Someone Else
Over Caring What People Think

Jealousy

You see yourself as..	Visualisation - See yourself as..
• Often getting jealous about at what other people have.	• Not needing to compare yourself to others. • Being satisfied with what you have. • Right now all is okay.

SEE RELATED TOPICS

Jealousy
What Makes Happy People
Right Now I am OK
Explore Solutions
Do Your Best & Acceptance
Be Truthful & Honest
Be Humble
Accept Your Shadow
You Can Only Control So Much
Forgive Yourself
Judging & Self Reflection
Being the Victim
Negative Self-talk

Being Someone Else
Over Caring What People Think

Nervousness and Shyness

You see yourself as..	Visualisation - See yourself as..
<ul><li>Always being nervous and uncomfortable.</li><li>Blushing when you becomes centre of attention.</li><li>Tense and not enjoying life.</li></ul>	<ul><li>Relaxed and not troubled.</li><li>With self-worth and as good as anyone else.</li></ul>

SEE RELATED TOPICS

Right Now I am OK
Being Assertive
Self-affirmation & Be Proud of Yourself
Smile
Explore Solutions
Do Your Best & Acceptance
Help Others & Giving
Accept Your Shadow
You Can Only Control So Much
Forgive Yourself
Risk & Pain
Write It Down
Saying Sorry Too Much
Judging & Self Reflection

Being the Victim
Negative Self-talk
Being Someone Else
Over Caring What People Think

Hate your Job or Life

You see yourself as..	Visualisation - See yourself as..
<ul><li>Unhappy, bored and stressed.</li><li>None fore-filled and unrewarded.</li><li>Being under appreciated.</li><li>Unchallenged.</li></ul>	<ul><li>Setting goals and planning where you want to be.</li><li>Being where you would like to be.</li><li>Taking little and frequent steps to stick to your plan and achieve your goal.</li><li>Taking up new challenges.</li><li>Enjoying any exercise.</li></ul>

SEE RELATED TOPICS

What Makes Happy People
Right Now I am OK
Self-affirmation & Be Proud of Yourself
Smile

Explore Solutions
Do Your Best & Acceptance
Accept Your Shadow
You Can Only Control So Much
Write It Down
Learn From Mistakes
Over Thinking The Future
Judging & Self Reflection
Negative Self-talk
Jealousy

Always Worrying About What Others Think

You see yourself as..	Visualisation - See yourself as..
- Always worrying about what people think about you.	- Realising that most people spend most of the time thinking about themselves.

SEE RELATED TOPICS

Over Caring What People Think
What Makes Happy People
Right Now I am OK
Being Assertive
Lending & Borrowing & Favours
Self-affirmation & Be Proud of Yourself
Smile
Explore Solutions
Do Your Best & Acceptance
Help Others & Giving
Empathy & Walk In Their Shoes
You Can Only Control So Much
Forgive Yourself
Forgive Others & Let go of Anger & Hate
Letting Go & Drop Burdens

Write It Down
Arguments & Less Emotion
Texting & Impulse Communication
Saying Sorry Too Much
Judging & Self Reflection
Being the Victim
Negative Self-talk
Being Someone Else

No Time and Rushing

You see yourself as..	Visualisation - See yourself as..
• Never having time to do what you want are life is zipping by without happiness.	• Starting and working on being mindful. • Planning and making "me" time and using it. • Doing the things you would like to do. • Decreasing the things you don't like to do. • Reflecting and affirming the things you have done that were for "me".

SEE RELATED TOPICS

Right Now I am OK
Self-affirmation & Be Proud of Yourself
Explore Solutions
Do Your Best & Acceptance
Addiction & Habits

You Can Only Control So Much
Write It Down
Over Thinking The Future
Judging & Self Reflection
Rushing

Fear

You see yourself as..	Visualisation - See yourself as..
• Fearing many events, situations and changing. Common fears like meeting people, conducting presentations, flying, not having money and so forth.	• Breaking the challenges into parts and slowly attacking each one.. • Doing it face the fear. • Accepting you have the fear and you will avoid it. • Exploring solutions with others.

SEE RELATED TOPICS

Right Now I am OK
Smile
Do Your Best & Acceptance
Accept Your Shadow
You Can Only Control So Much
Forgive Yourself
Risk & Pain
Write It Down
Over Thinking The Future

Procrastination
Judging & Self Reflection
Negative Self-talk
Being Someone Else

Big Challenges & Breaking Bad Habits

You see yourself as..	Visualisation - See yourself as..
<ul><li>Completely blocked and frozen by big challenges.</li><li>Always struggling financially.</li><li>With bad habits that you can never break.</li></ul>	<ul><li>Cutting the challenges into small pieces. and plan - for instance creating a budget.</li><li>Starting anywhere and soon.</li><li>Doing a little everyday and having targets.</li><li>Exploring solutions with other people.</li><li>The grand scheme of things.</li></ul>

SEE RELATED TOPICS

What Makes Happy People
Right Now I am OK
Being Assertive

Self-affirmation & Be Proud of Yourself
Smile
Explore Solutions
Do Your Best & Acceptance
Addiction & Habits
You Can Only Control So Much
Forgive Yourself
Letting Go & Drop Burdens
Write It Down
Learn From Mistakes
Over Thinking The Future
Procrastination
Judging & Self Reflection
Negative Self-talk

Resentment & Hate

You see yourself as..	Visualisation - See yourself as..
• Spending much time resenting or hating people causing ill feelings.	• Stopping wasting your time on hate and resentment you are only hurting yourself and no one else. • Letting go. • Forgiving others.

SEE RELATED TOPICS

What Makes Happy People
Being Assertive
Lending & Borrowing & Favours
Smile
Do Your Best & Acceptance
Help Others & Giving
Be Truthful & Honest
Empathy & Walk In Their Shoes
You Can Only Control So Much
Forgive Yourself
Forgive Others & Let go of Anger & Hate
Letting Go & Drop Burdens

- Write It Down
- Arguments & Less Emotion
- Texting & Impulse Communication
- Over Thinking The Future
- Saying Sorry Too Much
- Judging & Self Reflection
- Being the Victim
- Negative Self-talk
- Jealousy
- Over Caring What People Think

Worry About The Future

You see yourself as..	Visualisation - See yourself as..
- Spending much time worrying about what the future may bring.	- Not worrying about the future, the only thing we can predict about the future is that it is "uncertain". - Being mindful. - Right now I am okay. - Accepting whatever the future might bring.

SEE RELATED TOPICS

Right Now I am OK
Lending & Borrowing & Favours
Self-affirmation & Be Proud of Yourself
Explore Solutions
Do Your Best & Acceptance
You Can Only Control So Much
Forgive Yourself
Forgive Others & Let go of Anger & Hate

Letting Go & Drop Burdens
Risk & Pain
Write It Down
Time Heals
Learn From Mistakes
Over Thinking The Future
Saying Sorry Too Much
Procrastination
Judging & Self Reflection
Negative Self-talk
Jealousy
Being Someone Else
Over Caring What People Think

Not Liking Yourself

You see yourself as..	Visualisation - See yourself as..
- Not liking yourself, what you do and how you behave.	- Forgiving yourself. - Affirming your good qualities. - Being humble. - Accepting that about a third of people wont like you, one third don't care and concentrate on that final third who do. - Addressing the issues you don't like by using this book.

SEE RELATED TOPICS

What Makes Happy People
Right Now I am OK
Self-affirmation & Be Proud of Yourself
Smile
Explore Solutions
Do Your Best & Acceptance
Accept Your Shadow

You Can Only Control So Much
Letting Go & Drop Burdens
Risk & Pain
Write It Down
Over Thinking The Future
Judging & Self Reflection
Being the Victim
Negative Self-talk
Jealousy
Being Someone Else
Over Caring What People Think

Meeting Targets or Goals

You see yourself as..	Visualisation - See yourself as..
- Not being able to meet your targets or goals and fear the repercussions.	- Only being able to do your best and do it. - Relieving the stress by telling someone that you are concerned with attaining the target or goal.

SEE RELATED TOPICS

Right Now I am OK
Being Assertive
Self-affirmation & Be Proud of Yourself
Smile
Explore Solutions
Do Your Best & Acceptance
Addiction & Habits
You Can Only Control So Much
Forgive Yourself
Letting Go & Drop Burdens
Write It Down
Learn From Mistakes
Over Thinking The Future

Judging & Self Reflection
Negative Self-talk

Getting Old

You see yourself as..	Visualisation - See yourself as..
• Getting old, not looking good and that health is slowly failing.	• Living youthfully. • Welcoming and accepting your ageing looks and the experience it reflects. • Accepting we ALL get old and each of us has their time. • Living as healthily as you can. • Enjoying every moment you have and being mindful. • Age is something we cannot control so we must accept it.

SEE RELATED TOPICS

What Makes Happy People
Right Now I am OK
Self-affirmation & Be Proud of Yourself
Smile
Explore Solutions
Do Your Best & Acceptance
Accept Your Shadow
You Can Only Control So Much
Forgive Yourself
Letting Go & Drop Burdens
Risk & Pain
Over Thinking The Future
Judging & Self Reflection
Negative Self-talk
Being Someone Else

Not Being Attractive

You see yourself as..	Visualisation - See yourself as..
- Being ugly, less attractive than others and odd.	- Accepting as there is little you can do it is something we have little control of. - Making the most out of what you have, like makeup, clothes, surgery, losing weight and so forth. - Realising that you can change the most important aspect of being attractive, your personality. - Being attractive as you would like to be. - Being attractive in the big scheme of things is not so important. - Affirming your

- good points.
- Not comparing how attractive you are with others.
- Smiling and laughing as people find it attractive.

SEE RELATED TOPICS

What Makes Happy People
Right Now I am OK
Self-affirmation & Be Proud of Yourself
Smile
Explore Solutions
Do Your Best & Acceptance
Be Truthful & Honest
Be Humble
Accept Your Shadow
You Can Only Control So Much
Forgive Yourself
Saying Sorry Too Much
Impulse Buying
Judging & Self Reflection
Negative Self-talk
Being Someone Else

Fear of Taking The First or Next Step

You see yourself as..	Visualisation - See yourself as..
• Needing to embark on change but fear the hard work, discomfort, self-belief and strength.	• Being happy to embark on this new journey. • Feeling the discomfort but doing it any way. • Realising that few of us are "ready" or "fully prepared" but succeed anyway. "He who dares wins". • Being strong.

SEE RELATED TOPICS

Being Assertive
Do Your Best & Acceptance
Accept Your Shadow
Addiction & Habits
You Can Only Control So Much
Forgive Yourself
Write It Down

Learn From Mistakes
Over Thinking The Future
Procrastination
Negative Self-talk

Control and Acceptance

You see yourself as..	Visualisation - See yourself as..
<ul><li>Out of control.</li><li>Seeking perfection.</li><li>Stressed because of events occur out of your control.</li><li>Dissatisfied.</li></ul>	<ul><li>Accepting the events and issues that you have no control of.</li></ul>

SEE RELATED TOPICS

What Makes Happy People
Right Now I am OK
Self-affirmation & Be Proud of Yourself
Do Your Best & Acceptance
Accept Your Shadow
You Can Only Control So Much
Forgive Yourself
Letting Go & Drop Burdens
Risk & Pain
Write It Down
Time Heals
Over Thinking The Future
Impulse Buying
Judging & Self Reflection
Being the Victim

Negative Self-talk
Being Someone Else
Over Caring What People Think

Printed in Great Britain
by Amazon